THIS BOOK BELONGS TO:

_____

_____

Lists to Live By

Ellen Elliott

HARVEST HOUSE PUBLISHERS
EUGENE, OREGON

Cover design by Left Coast Design

Interior design by Janelle Coury

Illustration by Ellen Elliott

Lists to Live By

Copyright © 2018 Ellen Matkowski
Published by Harvest House Publishers
Eugene, Oregon 97408
www.harvesthousepublishers.com

ISBN 978-0-7369-7502-5 (hardcover)

Library of Congress Cataloging-in-Publication Data is on file at the Library of Congress, Washington, DC.

Printed in China

18 19 20 21 22 23 24 25 26 / RDS-JC / 10 9 8 7 6 5 4 3 2 1

FOR LOVE OF LISTS

I love making lists!

My love for list making began when I was young. I have memories of creating lists of clothing my Barbie desperately needed. I was not above ranking my stuffed animals from best to worst. And, let me tell you, my Christmas wish lists were *epic*. I'd pull out the Sears toy catalog, and before long, my list had color-coordinated, itemized footnotes and diagrams.

As adulthood brought new responsibilities and obligations, my list-making habit matured. Gone were the pink Barbie wardrobe lists, only to be replaced with notebooks full of grocery, errand, and baby-name lists. Lists helped take all the ideas and tasks percolating in my head and pin them down on a sheet of paper, all crisp and organized. A good list can do wonders. It can take a mind of fragmented thoughts and turn them into an ordered plan of action or a cohesive idea. A list can add focus to your day and open your mind to exciting new possibilities.

So I got to thinking: What if we took the same energy and imagination we spend on our weekly errand list and applied it to our relationship with our heavenly Father? Practicing and refining our faith every day keeps our walk with God fresh and vital. We can pour into that relationship in a myriad of ways, including studying the Bible, praying, and journaling. Let's add list making to the mix!

I hope you find joy and inspiration in *Lists to Live By*. I challenge you to stretch your imagination! Use this book in a way that best suits your lifestyle. Write in it methodically from the beginning or pick a random page every day. Work through it by yourself or in a weekly group setting. It's up to you! My prayer for you is that *Lists to Live By* can be a creative blessing in your life as you explore list after list.

By faith we understand that the entire universe was formed at God's command, that what we now see did not come from anything that can be seen.

HEBREWS 11:3

List some aspects of God's creation that always astound you.

_____

_____

_____

_____

_____

_____

_____

_____

_____

_____

BRINGING THE LIST TO LIFE

Where in nature do you feel closest to God?
How can you carve out more time in your schedule to go there?

Don't worry about anything; instead,
pray about everything. Tell God what you need,
and thank him for all he has done.

PHILIPPIANS 4:6

Lists things you often worry about...and
should consider bringing to God.

_____

_____

_____

_____

_____

_____

_____

_____

_____

_____

BRINGING THE LIST TO LIFE

Write your worries on slips of paper, give them to God, and
place them in a prayer box. If you start worrying about these
things again, remember that you already gave them to God!

3

I will praise God's name with singing,
and I will honor him with thanksgiving.
PSALM 69:30

List your favorite worship songs.

_____

_____

_____

_____

_____

_____

_____

_____

_____

_____

_____

_____

_____

_____

BRINGING THE LIST TO LIFE
Which specific lyrics have meant the most to you?
Consider sharing on social media.

A cheerful heart is good medicine,
but a broken spirit saps a person's strength.
PROVERBS 17:22

List ways God brings joyful laughter into your life.

_____

_____

_____

_____

_____

_____

_____

_____

_____

_____

_____

PRAYER

Lord, help me to look for the lighthearted
moments in life—and embrace them.

5

Be thankful in all circumstances, for this is God's will for you who belong to Christ Jesus.
1 THESSALONIANS 5:18

List the blessings in your life you are most thankful for.

_____

_____

_____

_____

_____

_____

_____

_____

_____

_____

_____

_____

_____

_____

_____

_____

_____

_____

_____

_____

_____

_____

_____

_____

_____

_____

_____

_____

_____

_____

BRINGING THE LIST TO LIFE
This week, try to begin every prayer with a thank-you to God.

6

For the LORD is good.
His unfailing love continues forever,
and his faithfulness continues to each generation.
PSALM 100:5

List key truths you would like to pass on to your own kids—or any children in your life.

_____

_____

_____

_____

_____

_____

_____

_____

_____

_____

_____

_____

_____

_____

_____

_____

_____

_____

_____

_____

_____

_____

_____

_____

_____

_____

_____

_____

_____

PRAYER

Lord, help me to share Your truths with the next generation.

7

The heartfelt counsel of a friend
is as sweet as perfume and incense.
PROVERBS 27:9

List friends who bring goodness into your life.

_____

_____

_____

_____

_____

_____

_____

_____

_____

_____

_____

_____

_____

BRINGING THE LIST TO LIFE

Of all the friends on this list, who have you known the longest?
Contact this friend and thank him or her for being part of your life.

Come close to God, and God will come close to you.
JAMES 4:8

List habits that help you draw near to God.

_____

_____

_____

_____

_____

_____

_____

_____

_____

_____

_____

BRINGING THE LIST TO LIFE

Write out a plan for spending time with God every day. Of course,
"life" often interferes with our plans for spiritual growth.
What will you do to keep your plan on track?

9

Whatever you do, do well.
Ecclesiastes 9:10

List new skills you would like to learn
(or dormant skills you would like to sharpen).

_____

_____

_____

_____

_____

_____

_____

_____

_____

_____

BRINGING THE LIST TO LIFE

What special skill do you already possess?
How can you use this ability for God's glory?

If you need wisdom, ask our generous God,
and he will give it to you.
He will not rebuke you for asking.

JAMES 1:5

List times you doubted but God showed up anyway.

_____

_____

_____

_____

_____

_____

_____

_____

_____

_____

_____

_____

_____

_____

_____

_____

_____

_____

_____

_____

_____

_____

_____

_____

_____

_____

_____

_____

BRINGING THE LIST TO LIFE

In what area of your life are you currently experiencing doubt?
What can you do to more fully turn that doubt over to God?

11

Yes, joyful are those who live like this!
Joyful indeed are those whose God is the LORD.
PSALM 144:15

List daily blessings that make you happy.

_____

_____

_____

_____

_____

_____

_____

_____

_____

_____

_____

_____

_____

_____

_____

_____

_____

_____

_____

_____

_____

_____

_____

_____

_____

_____

_____

_____

BRINGING THE LIST TO LIFE
Begin a daily gratitude journal to
help keep you focused on your blessings.

12

If you look for me wholeheartedly, you will find me.
JEREMIAH 29:13

Modern life can become so frantic and busy.
List some ways you can seek the Lord's presence
and wisdom, even during your most hectic days.

_____

_____

_____

_____

_____

_____

_____

_____

_____

_____

_____

_____

_____

_____

_____

_____

_____

_____

_____

_____

_____

_____

_____

_____

_____

_____

_____

_____

_____

_____

_____

PRAYER
Lord, remind me of Your presence throughout my day.

13

This is my command—be strong and courageous!
Do not be afraid or discouraged. For the Lord
your God is with you wherever you go.
Joshua 1:9

List places you'd like to visit.

_____

_____

_____

_____

_____

_____

_____

_____

_____

_____

_____

_____

_____

BRINGING THE LIST TO LIFE
What is a favorite place you've visited?
What made it so special to you?

14

Two people are better off than one, for they can help each other succeed. If one person falls, the other can reach out and help. But someone who falls alone is in real trouble.
ECCLESIASTES 4:9-10

List times when you've been given a helping hand.

_____

_____

_____

_____

_____

_____

_____

_____

_____

_____

_____

_____

_____

_____

_____

_____

_____

_____

_____

_____

_____

_____

_____

_____

_____

_____

_____

_____

_____

PRAYER

Lord, thank You for sending others to care
for me when I needed them.

15

Yes, the LORD has done amazing things for us!
What joy!
PSALM 126:3

List some great things God has done in your family.

_____

_____

_____

_____

_____

_____

_____

_____

_____

_____

_____

_____

_____

_____

BRINGING THE LIST TO LIFE

Describe a time when you clearly saw God
at work in the life of a family member.

16

Do not waste time arguing over godless ideas and old wives' tales. Instead, train yourself to be godly.
1 TIMOTHY 4:7

List some small scheduling changes that could make a big impact on your daily attitude and effectiveness.

_____

_____

_____

_____

_____

_____

_____

_____

_____

_____

_____

17

Wait patiently for the LORD.
Be brave and courageous.
Yes, wait patiently for the LORD.
PSALM 27:14

List some lessons you have learned while waiting on God.

_____

_____

_____

_____

_____

_____

_____

_____

_____

_____

_____

_____

_____

_____

_____

_____

_____

_____

_____

_____

_____

_____

_____

_____

_____

_____

_____

BRINGING THE LIST TO LIFE

Describe a time when God didn't work on your schedule,
but things worked out because of God's perfect timing.

18

Be sure to fear the LORD and faithfully serve him.
Think of all the wonderful things he has done for you.
1 SAMUEL 12:24

List some ways God has amazed you in your work or school life.

_____

_____

_____

_____

_____

_____

_____

_____

_____

_____

_____

PRAYER

Lord, help me to see Your ways in everything I do.

19

*In peace I will lie down and sleep,
for you alone, O LORD, will keep me safe.*
PSALM 4:8

List ways you could connect with God before bedtime.

_____

_____

_____

_____

_____

_____

_____

_____

_____

_____

_____

BRINGING THE LIST TO LIFE
Write your own special bedtime prayer.

20

Faith comes from hearing, that is, hearing the Good News about Christ.
ROMANS 10:17

List a few of your favorite Bible verses.

_____

_____

_____

_____

_____

_____

_____

_____

_____

_____

_____

_____

_____

_____

BRINGING THE LIST TO LIFE

Of all the verses listed above, which one is
most meaningful to you? Why?

21

Let us think of ways to motivate one another to acts of love and good works. And let us not neglect our meeting together, as some people do, but encourage one another, especially now that the day of his return is drawing near.

HEBREWS 10:24-25

List the ways your church family encourages and motivates you.

BRINGING THE LIST TO LIFE

What is your favorite part of your church worship service? Why?

22

I pray that God, the source of hope, will fill you completely with joy and peace because you trust in him. Then you will overflow with confident hope through the power of the Holy Spirit.
ROMANS 15:13

List some of your most joyful moments from childhood.

_____

_____

_____

_____

_____

_____

_____

_____

_____

_____

_____

_____

_____

_____

_____

_____

_____

_____

_____

_____

_____

_____

_____

_____

_____

_____

BRINGING THE LIST TO LIFE

Who was a favorite childhood friend? What did
you love about him or her? If you can, let this
friend know you are thankful for him or her.

23

Give all your worries and cares to God, for he cares about you.
1 PETER 5:7

List some fears about the future—
fears you need to turn over to God.

_____

_____

_____

_____

_____

_____

_____

_____

_____

_____

_____

_____

_____

_____

PRAYER

Lord, I know that my life and future are in Your big, strong hands.
Thank You for the peace this brings me.

24

Worry weighs a person down;
an encouraging word cheers a person up.
PROVERBS 12:25

List some kind words and compliments
that have built you up in the past.

BRINGING THE LIST TO LIFE

Choose a friend or family member and commit to
encouraging him or her this week.

25

You will know the truth,
and the truth will set you free.
John 8:32

List truths to cling to when you face a spiritual attack.

_____

_____

_____

_____

_____

_____

_____

_____

_____

_____

_____

_____

_____

_____

_____

_____

_____

_____

_____

_____

_____

_____

_____

_____

_____

_____

_____

_____

BRINGING THE LIST TO LIFE

Post these truths on your bathroom mirror. Let them help you
remember that no matter the struggle, God's got this!

26

Dear children, let's not merely say that we love each other; let us show the truth by our actions.
1 JOHN 3:18

List ways you can love and serve others in your neighborhood.

_____

_____

_____

_____

_____

_____

_____

_____

_____

_____

_____

_____

_____

BRINGING THE LIST TO LIFE

This week, reach out to a neighbor who might need a friend.

27

Show me the right path, O LORD;
point out the road for me to follow.
PSALM 25:4

List times you've felt like giving up
but God helped you persevere.

_____

_____

_____

_____

_____

_____

_____

_____

_____

_____

_____

_____

_____

_____

_____

_____

_____

_____

_____

_____

_____

_____

_____

_____

_____

_____

_____

_____

_____

PRAYER

Lord, I need Your strength to keep going every day.
Thank You for your steadfast power.

28

Keep on asking, and you will receive what you ask for. Keep on seeking, and you will find. Keep on knocking, and the door will be opened to you. For everyone who asks, receives. Everyone who seeks, finds. And to everyone who knocks, the door will be opened.

MATTHEW 7:7-8

List some prayers you haven't received an answer to...yet.

_____

_____

_____

_____

_____

_____

_____

_____

_____

_____

_____

_____

_____

_____

_____

_____

_____

_____

_____

_____

_____

_____

_____

_____

_____

_____

_____

PRAYER

Lord, I know You listen to me and have my best interests at heart.
Help me to be patient and watchful for Your responses.

29

*He heals the brokenhearted
and bandages their wounds.*
PSALM 147:3

List times when God has healed your broken heart.

_____

_____

_____

_____

_____

_____

_____

_____

_____

_____

_____

_____

_____

_____

_____

_____

_____

_____

_____

_____

_____

_____

_____

_____

_____

BRINGING THE LIST TO LIFE

Do you know someone who is experiencing loss or grief?
Make an effort to show them love this week.

30

Be strong and courageous! Do not be afraid and do not panic before them. For the LORD your God will personally go ahead of you. He will neither fail you nor abandon you.
DEUTERONOMY 31:6

List times you've been bold for Christ.

_____

_____

_____

_____

_____

_____

_____

_____

_____

_____

_____

BRINGING THE LIST TO LIFE

Imagine what would your life could look
like if you lived without fear.

31

Be still, and know that I am God!
I will be honored by every nation.
I will be honored throughout the world.
PSALM 46:10

List places where you find stillness.

_____

_____

_____

_____

_____

_____

_____

_____

_____

_____

_____

_____

BRINGING THE LIST TO LIFE

If you don't already have one,
find a quiet spot and make it your own.

32

Anyone who belongs to Christ has become a new person. The old life is gone; a new life has begun!
2 Corinthians 5:17

List ways God has transformed you.

_____

_____

_____

_____

_____

_____

_____

_____

_____

_____

_____

_____

_____

PRAYER

Lord, I praise You for continually
transforming me to be more like Jesus.

33

Thank You for making me so wonderfully complex!
Your workmanship is marvelous—how well I know it.
PSALM 139:14

List some special or unique talents God has given to you.

_____

_____

_____

_____

_____

_____

_____

_____

_____

_____

_____

_____

_____

_____

_____

_____

BRINGING THE LIST TO LIFE
Describe a time when God used your abilities for a specific purpose.

34

Store your treasures in heaven, where moths and rust cannot destroy, and thieves do not break in and steal. Wherever your treasure is, there the desires of your heart will also be.

MATTHEW 6:20-21

List items you could get rid of to lighten your load—
physically, mentally, or spiritually.

_____

_____

_____

_____

_____

_____

_____

_____

_____

_____

_____

BRINGING THE LIST TO LIFE

This week, donate a box or bag of items to
a charity or cause you believe in.

35

The Holy Spirit produces this kind of fruit in our lives: love, joy, peace, patience, kindness, goodness, faithfulness, gentleness, and self-control.

GALATIANS 5:22

List friends who embody
different aspects of the Spirit's fruit.

_____

_____

_____

_____

_____

_____

_____

_____

_____

_____

_____

_____

_____

_____

_____

_____

_____

_____

_____

_____

_____

_____

_____

_____

_____

PRAYER

Lord, thank You for giving me friends and loved ones—
and for the godly qualities they bring to life.

36

Give me neither poverty nor riches!
PROVERBS 30:8

List a few small luxuries you
could sacrifice to live more simply.

_____

_____

_____

_____

_____

_____

_____

_____

_____

_____

_____

_____

_____

_____

_____

_____

_____

_____

_____

_____

_____

_____

_____

_____

_____

_____

_____

_____

_____

BRINGING THE LIST TO LIFE

Describe a time when someone made a sacrifice for you.
How did it affect you? Is there someone
you can bless in a similar way?

37

I have been a constant example of how you
can help those in need by working hard.
You should remember the words of the Lord Jesus:
"It is more blessed to give than to receive."

ACTS 20:35

List some groups or organizations doing work you
could support with your time, talent, or money.

BRINGING THE LIST TO LIFE

This week, reach out to a local organization
and learn what you can do to help.

38

Don't you realize that your body is the temple of the Holy Spirit, who lives in you and was given to you by God? You do not belong to yourself, for God bought you with a high price. So you must honor God with your body.

1 CORINTHIANS 6:19-20

List qualities you love about the body God gave you.

_____

_____

_____

_____

_____

_____

_____

_____

_____

_____

_____

BRINGING THE LIST TO LIFE

This month, try a new activity—something that is both intriguing and challenging.

39

I will meditate on your majestic, glorious splendor and your wonderful miracles.
Psalm 145:5

List places where you have felt God's majesty.

_____

_____

_____

_____

_____

_____

_____

_____

_____

_____

_____

_____

_____

_____

_____

_____

_____

_____

_____

_____

_____

_____

_____

_____

_____

_____

_____

BRINGING THE LIST TO LIFE
Find a photo of an inspiring place and make it
your cell phone background or computer screen saver.

40

He said, "My grace is all you need. My power works best in weakness." So now I am glad to boast about my weaknesses, so that the power of Christ can work through me.

2 CORINTHIANS 12:9

List times that God has
used your weaknesses for His glory.

_____

_____

_____

_____

_____

_____

_____

_____

_____

_____

_____

_____

PRAYER

Lord, I give all of me to You—
both my strengths and my weaknesses.

"I know the plans I have for you," says the LORD.
"They are plans for good and not for disaster,
to give you a future and a hope."

JEREMIAH 29:11

List times you were confused or without direction, but God showed you the way.

_____

_____

_____

_____

_____

_____

_____

_____

_____

_____

_____

_____

_____

_____

_____

_____

_____

_____

_____

_____

_____

_____

_____

_____

_____

_____

_____

_____

_____

_____

_____

PRAYER

Lord, You grant wisdom and peace when we ask for it.
Help me to trust You when the answers aren't clear.

42

As iron sharpens iron,
so a friend sharpens a friend.
PROVERBS 27:17

List the qualities you value in a true friend.

_____

_____

_____

_____

_____

_____

_____

_____

_____

_____

_____

_____

_____

BRINGING THE LIST TO LIFE

Describe friends who embody the qualities you listed above.

43

You must grow in the grace and knowledge of our Lord and Savior Jesus Christ.
2 Peter 3:18

List ways you've grown in your faith in the past year.

_____

_____

_____

_____

_____

_____

_____

_____

_____

_____

_____

_____

_____

_____

_____

_____

_____

_____

_____

_____

_____

_____

_____

_____

_____

_____

_____

_____

_____

BRINGING THE LIST TO LIFE

Write about a recent time you realized you
had experienced growth in Christ.

Do everything without complaining and arguing.
PHILIPPIANS 2:14

List ways you can have a happier heart
while doing chores you don't enjoy.

_____
_____
_____
_____
_____
_____
_____
_____
_____
_____
_____
_____
_____

BRINGING THE LIST TO LIFE

What activity have you been putting off for a while?
Try to tackle it with gusto today!

You were cleansed; you were made holy; you were made right with God by calling on the name of the Lord Jesus Christ and by the Spirit of our God.

1 Corinthians 6:11

List some character flaws God is trying
to remove from your life.

_____

_____

_____

_____

_____

_____

_____

_____

_____

_____

_____

_____

_____

_____

PRAYER

Lord, I know You love me exactly as I am.
Please work on my rough spots so I can be the best I can be.

46

I have hidden your word in my heart,
that I might not sin against you.
PSALM 119:11

List some new Bible verses you would like to memorize.

_____

_____

_____

_____

_____

_____

_____

_____

_____

_____

_____

_____

_____

BRINGING THE LIST TO LIFE

Write your new verses on notecards.
Ask an artist friend to help you decorate each one with extra flair.

47

What is the price of five sparrows—two copper coins? Yet God does not forget a single one of them.
LUKE 12:6

List pets that mean or have meant a great deal to you.

PRAYER

Lord, thank You for animals that have brought sweetness to my life.

48

Such things were written in the Scriptures long ago to teach us. And the Scriptures give us hope and encouragement as we wait patiently for God's promises to be fulfilled.

ROMANS 15:4

When it comes to struggles and challenges, which Bible characters do you relate to most?

_____

_____

_____

_____

_____

_____

_____

_____

_____

BRINGING THE LIST TO LIFE

Pick someone from your list and reread his or her story. How did God help this person through hardships?

49

Study this Book of Instruction continually. Meditate on it day and night so you will be sure to obey everything written in it. Only then will you prosper and succeed in all you do.

JOSHUA 1:8

List some creative ways you could try to memorize Bible verses. (If you get stuck, look for ideas online or ask a teacher.)

_____

_____

_____

_____

_____

_____

_____

_____

_____

_____

_____

BRINGING THE LIST TO LIFE

Pick a Scripture and try to memorize it this week.

50

Anyone with ears to hear should listen and understand.
MARK 4:23

List your favorite parables of Jesus.

_____

_____

_____

_____

_____

_____

_____

_____

_____

_____

_____

_____

_____

_____

_____

_____

_____

_____

_____

_____

_____

_____

_____

_____

_____

BRINGING THE LIST TO LIFE

Write your own unique parable for modern times.
Consider sharing it with friends or family members.

51

Let the heavens be glad, and the earth rejoice!
Let the sea and everything in it shout his praise!
PSALM 96:11

List examples of where you see God's design in nature.

_____

_____

_____

_____

_____

_____

_____

_____

_____

_____

_____

_____

_____

_____

_____

BRINGING THE LIST TO LIFE

In the next few days, take a long walk and
admire the beauty of God's creation.

52

Work willingly at whatever you do, as though you were working for the Lord rather than for people.
COLOSSIANS 3:23

List ways you express your creativity.

_____

_____

_____

_____

_____

_____

_____

_____

_____

_____

_____

_____

_____

_____

_____

_____

_____

_____

_____

_____

_____

_____

_____

_____

_____

_____

_____

_____

_____

BRINGING THE LIST TO LIFE

Pick an activity from your list and spend
an afternoon getting creative!

53

Look at the lilies of the field and how they grow.
They don't work or make their clothing, yet Solomon in
all his glory was not dressed as beautifully as they are.

MATTHEW 6:28-29

List some of your favorite flowers or plants.

54

Encourage each other and build each other up, just as you are already doing.
1 Thessalonians 5:11

List people who could use an encouraging word this week.

_____

_____

_____

_____

_____

_____

_____

_____

_____

_____

_____

_____

_____

_____

_____

_____

_____

_____

_____

_____

_____

_____

_____

_____

_____

_____

BRINGING THE LIST TO LIFE

This week, reach out to someone on your list
and encourage him or her.

55

*She is clothed with strength and dignity,
and she laughs without fear of the future.*
PROVERBS 31:25

List positive attributes of your mother
or a maternal figure in your life.

_____

_____

_____

_____

_____

_____

_____

_____

_____

_____

_____

_____

_____

_____

_____

BRINGING THE LIST TO LIFE

Write and send a thank-you note to this cherished person.
(You might find this activity helpful even if the person has passed.)

56

The godly walk with integrity;
blessed are their children who follow them.
PROVERBS 20:7

List positive attributes of your father
or a paternal figure in your life.

_____

_____

_____

_____

_____

_____

_____

_____

_____

_____

_____

_____

_____

_____

_____

_____

_____

_____

_____

_____

_____

_____

_____

_____

_____

_____

_____

_____

_____

_____

BRINGING THE LIST TO LIFE

Write and send a thank-you note to this beloved person.
(You might find this activity helpful even if the person has passed.)

57

Joyful is the person who finds wisdom,
the one who gains understanding.
PROVERBS 3:13

List several books that have helped you grow spiritually.

_____

_____

_____

_____

_____

_____

_____

_____

_____

_____

_____

_____

_____

_____

_____

_____

BRINGING THE LIST TO LIFE

Consider starting a book club, or joining one,
to share insights with others.

58

Let the message about Christ, in all its richness, fill your lives. Teach and counsel each other with all the wisdom he gives.
Colossians 3:16

List some favorite quotes from Christian leaders.

_____

_____

_____

_____

_____

_____

_____

_____

_____

_____

_____

_____

_____

_____

PRAYER

Lord, bless and help those who lead in schools,
in communities, and in nations around the globe.

59

For everything there is a season,
a time for every activity under heaven.
ECCLESIASTES 3:1

List the reasons why you love your favorite season.

_____

_____

_____

_____

_____

_____

_____

_____

_____

_____

_____

_____

_____

_____

BRINGING THE LIST TO LIFE
Lord, thank You for guiding me through all seasons of life.

Direct your children onto the right path,
and when they are older, they will not leave it.
PROVERBS 22:6

List a few objects that remind you of your childhood.

_____

_____

_____

_____

_____

_____

_____

_____

_____

_____

_____

_____

_____

_____

_____

_____

_____

_____

_____

_____

_____

_____

_____

_____

_____

_____

_____

_____

_____

_____

_____

BRINGING THE LIST TO LIFE
Recall the happiest time in your childhood. What made it so joyful?

All praise to God, the Father of our Lord Jesus Christ. It is by his great mercy that we have been born again, because God raised Jesus Christ from the dead.

1 PETER 1:3

List your favorite Easter memories.

_____

_____

_____

_____

_____

_____

_____

_____

_____

_____

_____

_____

_____

_____

_____

_____

_____

_____

_____

_____

_____

_____

_____

_____

_____

_____

_____

BRINGING THE LIST TO LIFE

Describe a time when God gave you a period of renewal.
Could sharing this experience help someone you know?

62

Plans go wrong for lack of advice;
many advisers bring success.
PROVERBS 15:22

List people who helped mold you into who you are.

_____

_____

_____

_____

_____

_____

_____

_____

_____

_____

_____

_____

_____

_____

PRAYER

Lord, thank You for all the loved ones who have
supported me and helped shape my character.

63

Always be full of joy in the Lord.
I say it again—rejoice!
PHILIPPIANS 4:4

List friends who make you laugh.

_____

_____

_____

_____

_____

_____

_____

_____

_____

_____

_____

_____

_____

_____

_____

BRINGING THE LIST TO LIFE

How can you bring more joy and laughter to your friendships?
Put your ideas into action this week.

64

You made all the delicate, inner parts of my body and knit me together in my mother's womb.
PSALM 139:13

List things about you nobody else knows but God.

65

Without wise leadership, a nation falls;
there is safety in having many advisers.
PROVERBS 11:14

List the best advice you've received from trusted Christian mentors.

_____

_____

_____

_____

_____

_____

_____

_____

_____

_____

_____

_____

_____

_____

_____

_____

_____

_____

_____

_____

_____

_____

_____

_____

_____

_____

_____

_____

_____

PRAYER

Lord, thank You for providing me with godly wisdom
from people who have gone before me.

66

May the words of my mouth
and the meditation of my heart
be pleasing to you,
O LORD, my rock and my redeemer.
PSALM 19:14

List some of your favorite words.

_____

_____

_____

_____

_____

_____

_____

_____

_____

_____

_____

_____

_____

_____

_____

_____

_____

_____

_____

_____

_____

_____

_____

_____

_____

_____

_____

_____

BRINGING THE LIST TO LIFE

This week, be extra mindful of your thoughts,
because our thoughts often become our words.

67

God blesses those who patiently endure testing and temptation. Afterward they will receive the crown of life that God has promised to those who love him.

JAMES 1:12

List the toughest decisions
God has helped you make.

_____

_____

_____

_____

_____

_____

_____

_____

_____

_____

_____

_____

_____

_____

_____

_____

_____

_____

_____

_____

_____

_____

_____

_____

_____

_____

_____

BRINGING THE LIST TO LIFE

What obstacles did you have to overcome to make those decisions?
What did you learn about yourself and your faith in the process?

68

*Whatever is good and perfect is
a gift coming down to us from God our Father,
who created all the lights in the heavens.*
JAMES 1:17

List the best gifts you've ever received.

_____

_____

_____

_____

_____

_____

_____

_____

_____

_____

_____

_____

_____

BRINGING THE LIST TO LIFE

What are some thoughtful, handmade gifts you could make
for others? Commit to creating a unique gift for someone this year.

69

When you are praying, first forgive anyone you are holding a grudge against, so that your Father in heaven will forgive your sins, too.

MARK 11:25

List a few memorable times when you have apologized and asked for forgiveness.

_____

_____

_____

_____

_____

_____

_____

_____

_____

_____

_____

_____

_____

_____

_____

_____

_____

_____

_____

_____

_____

_____

_____

_____

_____

BRINGING THE LIST TO LIFE

Are you harboring any resentment toward another person?
Is it time to finally forgive?

70

Those who live in the shelter of the Most High will find rest in the shadow of the Almighty.
PSALM 91:1

List times when God has sheltered you from a storm.

PRAYER

Lord, help me to trust that You will always
sustain me through stormy times.

71

Children are a gift from the LORD;
they are a reward from him.
PSALM 127:3

List some favorite childhood books.

_____

_____

_____

_____

_____

_____

_____

_____

_____

_____

_____

_____

_____

_____

_____

_____

_____

_____

_____

_____

_____

_____

_____

_____

_____

_____

_____

BRINGING THE LIST TO LIFE

Pick one of your special books and read it to a child this week.

72

There is more than enough room in my Father's home. If this were not so, would I have told you that I am going to prepare a place for you?
JOHN 14:2

List ways you could make your home more welcoming.

_____

_____

_____

_____

_____

_____

_____

_____

_____

_____

_____

_____

_____

_____

_____

_____

_____

_____

_____

_____

_____

_____

_____

_____

_____

_____

_____

_____

_____

_____

_____

BRINGING THE LIST TO LIFE

Do you have a friend you would like to know better?
Invite that person for a visit this week.

73

A friend is always loyal,
and a brother is born to help in time of need.
PROVERBS 17:17

List friends with whom you'd like to reconnect in a meaningful way.

_____

_____

_____

_____

_____

_____

_____

_____

_____

_____

_____

_____

_____

_____

_____

_____

_____

BRINGING THE LIST TO LIFE
Write a letter to a person you miss having in your life.

74

A child is born to us, a son is given to us.
The government will rest on his shoulders.
And he will be called:
Wonderful Counselor, Mighty God,
Everlasting Father, Prince of Peace.
ISAIAH 9:6

List your favorite Christmas traditions.

_____

_____

_____

_____

_____

_____

_____

_____

_____

_____

_____

_____

_____

BRINGING THE LIST TO LIFE

What can you do to make Christ the focus
during the next holiday season?

75

You are my safe refuge,
a fortress where my enemies cannot reach me.
PSALM 61:3

List the times in life when you've felt coziest,
as if God had wrapped you in His strong arms.

_____

_____

_____

_____

_____

_____

_____

_____

_____

_____

_____

_____

_____

_____

PRAYER

Lord, when life comes charging at me, You are my hiding place.

ANOTHER GREAT INTERACTIVE JOURNAL FROM HARVEST HOUSE PUBLISHERS

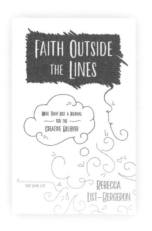

Create Space for Your Faith to Grow

If you're ready for the next fun step in journaling, this book is for you. Filled with faith-affirming activities to nurture your heart, mind, and soul, *Faith Outside the Lines* is the creative pursuit you have been craving.

Following God is anything but boring. Celebrate that truth when you apply your own unique personality to complete thought-provoking prompts, such as...

- Cover this page in love—using words, pictures symbols, scents...or anything!
- Fill this page with blessings. Then count 'em all up.
- When you see the word "God," what comes to mind? Fill in this page with your thoughts, feelings, and prayers.

These and many more engaging ideas await you in this unique interactive journal. Throughout, you'll also encounter Scripture verses and quotes to delight and inspire you.

Accept this invitation to go outside the lines and discover a deeper connection with our God of creativity and love.

To learn more about Harvest House books and
to read sample chapters, visit our website:

www.harvesthousepublishers.com

HARVEST HOUSE PUBLISHERS
EUGENE, OREGON
